31 days ways

2 pray 4 families

A monthly prayer guide to aid intercession
for families dealing with
mental illnesses

Catherine P. Downing

Author of *Sparks of Redemptive Grace*

Scripture quotations are from The Holy Bible, English Standard Version® (ESV®), copyright © 2001 by Crossway, a publishing ministry of Good News Publishers. Used by permission. All rights reserved.

All statistics are from the National Alliance on Mental Illness. **www.nami.org**

Printed in the United States of America
ISBN: 978-1-7324046-0-1

HISPUBLISHING GROUP

Division of Human Improvement Specialists, LLC
www.hispubg.com | *info@hispubg.com*

PREFACE

Like all families that are on a journey with mental illness, ours has at times been lonely and isolated. But as we became more transparent about our struggles, our caring and considerate community of faith began asking how they could help.

Our answer was always just one word: *pray*. In response to their question, *how?*, I prepared this list of ways to pray for our family in the daily ebb and flow of caring for a loved one with mental health difficulties. We have many amazing examples of how God has answered their prayers, and we are overwhelmingly thankful to Him. But just as powerful has been the reassurance that we do not walk this journey alone. Their prayers are a beautiful example of how to "bear one another's burdens." And we are forever grateful.

INTRODUCTION

"Pray for us."   1 Thessalonians 5:25

Families who walk alongside their loved ones in the labyrinths of mental illnesses are often hesitant to ask for prayer. They might feel others will judge them or their loved one, offer uninformed advice or initiate the gossip chain. But friends who are aware of their journey don't necessarily need specific details to pray effectively.

There are a few common concerns families always have and for which they always need God's provision for themselves and for their loved ones. This prayer guide provides prompts to help you pray each day effectively for them.

MENTAL ILLNESS, PRAYER, AND EXTRAVAGANT GRACE

I can't honestly say I am thankful for the mental illness that besets our son. But in full truthfulness I can say I am glad to have been forced to do battle with my theology of suffering and to test both its mettle and mine.

One of the links welded into the armor of my faith has almost corroded more than once: prayer. Specifically, the mystery of prayer related to mental illness. Through the years, I have prayed and I have not prayed. Sometimes I have asked others to pray and sometimes I have not. Often I have disguised my wishful thinking as prayer, and more times than I want to admit, my prayers have been just "vain repetitions."

But in recent years my beliefs about prayer, tested on the battlefield of my son's mania and repaired in the infirmary of sweet stability, have settled into a courageous trust in the One whose love, power, and goodness are unfathomable and unstoppable.

Here are some prayer principles I now hold onto firmly as I pray through the challenges of our loved one's battle with mental illness.

First, because mental illnesses are brain disorders, I pray as I would for any other physical sickness.

Because God can and does heal bodies, I always pray for healing.

Because that healing often comes through medical and therapeutic means, I pray for doctors, counselors, and chemists.

Because healing is enhanced by intentional body-care, I pray for good rest, nutrition, and exercise.

Because in His providence, God doesn't always cure everyone, I pray for patience, wisdom, and enduring faith.

Prayer, I have learned, is an act of open-handed expectation.

Second, because "each day has enough trouble of its own" (Matthew 6:34), I pray every single day for God's favor and grace. Every morning I thank God in anticipation of His presence being with us every single moment—no matter how the day unfolds. At the close of the day I give thanks for the ways I have seen His goodness and mercy follow us on that particular day (Psalm 23:6). And of course, throughout the day are the ongoing conversations with our

Father in heaven who knows our son best
and loves him most.

Prayer, I have discovered, is a discipline of
unceasing watchfulness.

Third, because God invites us to ask,
seek and knock (Matthew 7:7), I keep asking, seeking and knocking. I ask for direction on how to help our son. I seek after his
healing and wholeness. I knock, expecting
mercy to answer. As I pray I am mindful
that I implore neither a stingy, grace-
hoarding deity nor an impotent wannabe
god. Instead I come as one welcomed into
the throne room of the Most High God, at
the invitation of His generous Spirit,
through the door opened by His Son.

Prayer, I have experienced, is an invitation
to worshipful confidence.

Fourth, because my own sins and limitations impede my life every bit as much as mental illness disrupts our son's, I pray for forgiveness and transformation. I see how our son is unaware of the ways mental illness clouds his judgment and blocks his opportunities, so I ask God to reveal my own blind spots.

Prayer, I have begun to understand, is a sacrifice of sincere humility.

Finally, because God draws near to those who draw near to Him, I am emboldened to express the reality of my wobbly faith ("I do believe, help my unbelief," as in Mark 9:24) and in doing so, I am able to rest in the truth that He alone is the giver and sustainer of life. Prayer places me close enough to God to "touch the hem of His garment" (Matthew 9:20-21), and there I find peace and hope.

Prayer, I have found, is the journey into extravagant grace.

In the end, as I've prayed through the sufferings of our family and of others, I've discovered that prayer isn't so much a mystery to be bewildered with as it is the anchor to be secured by. Prayer, indeed, is the tether that ties us to the only One who is loving enough to listen compassionately, the only One wise enough to answer rightly, the only One mighty enough to respond thoroughly and the only One kind enough to wait with us as His own goodness unfolds.

Mental Illness, Prayer, and Extravagant Grace
was originally written as a guest blog for Amy Simpson,
(author of *Troubled Minds: Mental Illness and the Church's Mission*) and posted on her site, 10/2/17.

DAY 1. PEACE

When crises come, caregivers can become overwhelmed with anxiety and concern. Each episode can present a different set of issues and behaviors, so new approaches may need to be developed. Fear, worry and confusion often stir up an oppressive cloud blurring good thinking and wise decisions.

Pray families will experience the presence and love of God that will drive out fear. Pray they will receive Christ's gift of peace, even amid the storm. Pray the fog will lift and they can make good desisions with confidence.

DAY 2. FINANCIAL RESOURCES

The financial burden of caring for a loved one dealing with a mental health difficulty cannot be overestimated. In addition to costs for medical care, there are, in some cases, expenses related to fines, legal fees, unconstrained spending sprees, accidents and property damages. It is not unusual for caregivers to exhaust their savings and jeopardize retirement funds so they can tend to the needs of their loved one.

Pray God will provide the resources for families to pay for these extraordinary expenses and that they will not be overwhelmed by the added financial responsibilities.

DAY 3. COMMUNITY

Many families go into hibernation mode when their loved one is experiencing a severe episode. They can feel isolated and emotionally spent. The oppression of stigma and resulting shame can cause families to hide from the very sources of encouragement and hope available. Pray God will bring people to come alongside to support them, comfort them and pray with them.

Pray caregivers will have the energy to reach out to local mental health support groups, or begin their own. Ask God how you can be a part of His redemptive grace for them during difficult times.

DAY 4. HEALING

Although there are no medical cures for most severe mental illnesses, there is always a spark of hope within families that their loved one will be healed. People of faith know that God can and does bring His supernatural healing to many. Therefore, we never stop asking Him to intervene and touch our loved one.

Join families in asking for such a miracle. Pray they will have eyes of faith that see the miracles of everyday victories. Pray they will not lose heart as they wait for God's timing and perfect plan for their loved one.

DAY 5. CHILDREN IN THE FAMILY

Whether they are siblings or offspring, children are the forgotten. They are often overlooked when adults are trying desperately to cope with the mentally ill family member. However, in addition to the normal needs of childhood, those exposed to the behaviors of others dealing with mental illness have an additional layer of trauma and anxiety.

Pray those who are responsible to care for the children will stay aware of and be able to meet their needs. Pray the children will be protected from finding attention in unhealthy or unsafe ways from others who could do them harm.

DAY 6. PROTECTION

Those who deal with mental health difficulties are often victims of exploitation, abuse and crime. When severely depressed, there is an increased possibility that they will try to harm themselves. When in the grip of mania or psychosis, there may be increased aggression or high-risk behaviors.

Join families in praying that God will surround their loved ones with His angels. Pray He will direct them to safe places and caring people. Pray for protection of caregivers and others in the rare times when the ill family member may be violent or abusive.

DAY 7. WISDOM

The mental health systems in most places are inadequate, complex and difficult for family members to access. Family members need wisdom regarding what kind of help to look for and where to get it. The treatment or medication that was effective before may not be the right approach in the current situation.

Pray caregivers will find the exact kind of help they need at the specific time they need it. Pray local resources will have useful information and will be responsive to inquiries.

DAY 8. COMPANIONSHIP

Ignorance and stigma are just two reasons many people don't reach out in friendship to those dealing with mental illnesses. As a result, loneliness and isolation compound their needs. It is common for families to be the only source of companionship for their loved ones. This takes a toll on relationships and adds to the burden of caregivers.

Pray with the families that others will bring friendship and build community with their family member. Pray the loved one will be willing to participate in peer support groups. Pray churches will become places of acceptance and inclusion.

DAY 9. MEDICAL CARE

In the last 20 years there have been great advancements in pharmaceutical treatments for mental disorders. But there is no perfect medication. Many have unrelenting side effects. Others lose their efficacy quickly. Some work only in tandem with other medications, so there can be a complex combination of drugs. For those reasons and others, there is often resistance or non-compliance in taking medications. But when the right drugs are found and are taken, the results can be spectacular.

Pray with families that the most effective treatments can be found for their loved ones and there will be a willingness to take—and keep taking—the medications.

DAY 10. FORGIVENESS

A lot can go wrong in a family dealing with mental health difficulties. Harsh words, broken promises and destructive actions can shred trust and build thick barriers between family members. Over time offences stack up and block opportunities to serve one another in love.

Pray God will pour forgiveness generously upon each person in the family—forgiveness for each other, and for themselves. Pray a spirit of forbearance and grace will create a healthy environment of kindness and love. Pray there may be an abundance of grace when a loved one is unable to see how their behaviors impact others.

DAY 11. DUAL DIAGNOSIS/ ADDICTIONS

It is estimated that at least 35 percent of those suffering with a mental disorder are also dealing with some sort of addiction issue. For families coping with a loved one who has a brain disorder and abuses alcohol or drugs, challenges compound exponentially. Destructive addictions with behaviors such as gambling, spending, sex, or pornography use, may also be present.

Pray for families to be able discern any addictions their loved one may be secretely dealing with and know how to approach it. Pray for the individual to see and acknowledge the addiction, and be willing to get treatment.

DAY 12. STIGMA

Throughout most of the world, mental illness is misunderstood and wrapped in superstition, naïve theology, or scary folk-lore. Those who struggle with mental illnesses and their families are commonly ostracized, feared or ignored. Stigma is a barrier that keeps many from seeking help and shuts off opportunites for healthy relationships.

Pray communities, families and churches can become educated so they are able to overcome stigmatizing those with mental illness and instead become compassionate, inclusive and supportive. Pray for advocacy groups to be successful in their education programs.

DAY 13. SPIRITUAL GROWTH

As with other aspects of life for those deal-ing with mental health difficulties, their spirituality and relationship with God can become muddled and confused. They rarely have the opportunity to experience a life-giving and encouraging spiritual communi-ty where they are accepted and belong. Even churches are often not welcoming to-ward those who deal with mental illnesses.

Pray for the Holy Spirit to work mightily to bring about salvation and sustained faith for all those touched by mental illnesses. Pray for opportunities to participate in Christian community and benefit from biblical teaching.

DAY 14. MEANINGFUL USE OF TIME

For those who suffer with severe mental illnesses, full-time work or frequent interaction with strangers may not be possible. How can their hours be spent in meaningful and productive ways? Families look for outlets for their loved ones to be useful, but few are available.

Pray for direction and creativity to discover good options. Pray for ministries and programs that offer safe places where those with mental disorders can belong and participate in meaningful activities. Pray for those dealing with mental illness to understand that their worth and value is not dependent on productivity.

DAY 15. HOUSING

Safe, affordable, sanitary, wholesome housing options are very limited for those disabled by mental illness. In fact, approximently 26% of homeless adults suffer with mental illnesses. For families caring for adult loved ones, the housing dilemma is an overwhelming challenge. So, often, families provide a place in their own homes. This means the families are always on caregiver duty.

Pray for families to find suitable and safe housing for their loved ones. If in their own homes, pray for strength, stamina and ongoing good relationships within the family. Pray for communities to find ways to address the issue of homelessness amid those dealing with mental illnesses.

DAY 16. GRIEF/LOSS

There is an undercurrent of sadness in families living with mental health issues. Families grieve as they watch illness steal the quality of life from their loved one. They mourn over the losses in their own lives as they release many of their own plans and dreams to care for their family member.

Pray God will show them the ways He is caring for and blessing their loved one. Pray for comfort and for daily joys that can lift their spirits. Pray they will be able to let go of their own expectations without bitterness or resentment. Pray they will find hope and contentment in Him.

DAY 17. COMMUNICATION

Clear, constructive communication is often the key tool a caregiver needs to help a loved one through a difficult episode. However, each individual and situation requires a unique approach. Choice of words, tone of voice and timing of conversation combine to create a complex communication map.

Pray caregivers will listen with discernment to what their loved ones are trying to express. Pray for wisdom in how and when to respond. Pray those with many voices in their minds will be able to listen to good counsel from those who love them and be able to know the gracious love of God.

DAY 18. SELF-CARE

Those who care for loved ones struggling with mental illnesses also struggle with taking care of themselves. Continual demands for attentiveness and the need to be on constant alert take their toll. Caregiving has to be approached as a marathon, rather than a sprint, and those who run the race must find the right pace.

Pray caregivers will develop and maintain good rest, exercise and eating habits. Ask God to provide healthy relationships, strong faith and clear thinking. Pray they will rightly discern their own needs amid the demanding needs of their loved ones.

DAY 19. GUILT

Second-guessing decisions, revisiting the past and taking on some level of blame for a loved one's mental illness are haunting companions for caregivers. Despite reassurances that brain disorders are biological conditions and not caused by others, it is hard to not wonder what one could have done to prevent their loved one's illness.

Pray for relief from these internal accusers. Pray family members will be able to rest in the comfort of a God who knows, who understands and who pours out His redemptive grace. Pray caregivers can help each other walk in freedom from guilt.

DAY 20. TRIGGERS

Episodes of mania, depression or psychosis don't just randomly appear. They usually are triggered by an event, stress, changes in routine or medication. Holidays, unexpected visitors, or losses can be especially difficult to navigate for those dealing with mental illnesses.

Pray families can help their loved ones identify their own triggers and have a good plan for dealing with possible scenarios in healthy ways. Pray caregivers have discernment to anticipate challenging situations for their loved ones and to also be wise in dealing with unexpected triggers.

DAY 21. BOUNDARIES

Mutual respect, personal space, interaction intervals and financial support are just some of the areas of life in which caregivers must "draw the line" to create a healthy environment for themselves and their loved one. However, in each family unit, there may be some members who need to set their own boundaries differently than others in the family.

Pray for wisdom in defining boundaries and consistency in keeping them. Pray for understanding and respect within the family when members have differing perspectives.

DAY 22. DISCERNMENT

There is no one right way to help a loved one who is dealing with depression, mania or psychosis. The volatile nature of some mental illnesses means that what was helpful yesterday may not be accepted today. Families have to continually assess their loved one's moods, cognitive capacities and medication compliance.

Pray family members will be able to understand the factors at play so they can make good intervention plans. Pray they can identify hidden issues such as addictions, paranoia or abuse. Pray their loved one will be willing to accept their counsel and treatment.

DAY 23. EXPECTATIONS

Caregivers must continually adjust their own expectations of their loved ones when they struggle with mood swings or daily stressors. Though hard to do, it is loving and supportive to exercise forbearance and patience when the loved one isn't sleeping (or is only sleeping), when irritability is acute or when social interactions are difficult.

Pray for family members to discern the need of the moment and respond with wisdom, grace and compassion. Pray they will be able to set reasonable requests of their loved ones and be able to be flexible when moods or capacities change.

DAY 24. IMPACT ON JOB

The unpredictable nature of some mental illnesses means that family members often miss work as they tend to their loved ones in crisis. There may be seasons of prolonged, round-the-clock caregiving after a hospitalization or prior to intervention.

Pray that caregivers will find support from their employers and flexibility in their jobs. Pray for good contingency plans and that others will be willing to help when needed. Ask God to give family members creative ways to earn income while caring for their loved ones.

DAY 25. ENDURANCE

Because there are currently no cures for major mental illnesses, families look at a probable future of lifelong caregiving. Emotional, spiritual, mental and physical stamina are required, as is an ongoing agility to adjust to the ever-changing moods and needs of loved ones.

Pray for family members to find a sustainable pace with opportunities to rest along the way. Pray for daily refreshment and peace. Pray they will not grow weary in caring for their loved ones. Ask God to send others to help carry the load.

DAY 26. REST

Worry robs caregivers of sleep. Keeping vigil to watch for suicide attempts is emotionally and physically exhausting. Considering options and making difficult decisions during a crisis is a heavy weight on heart and mind. Praying without ceasing requires the sustaining power of the Holy Spirit.

Ask God to grant family members restorative sleep and opportunities for emotional, spiritual and mental refreshment. Pray they will be able to see when extra rest is needed and be able to find ways to meet that need.

DAY 27. HEALTH

Good eating and sleeping patterns, personal hygiene care and treatment for medical issues are difficult for those who deal with mental illnesses. Eating disorders, unpredictable sleep patterns and disinterest in personal care make it challenging to attain or maintain good health. Caregivers work extra hard to help their loved ones get good nutrition and exercise, but it is often a battle.

Pray loved ones will respond to prompts from caregivers and will have access to nutritious food, safe places to sleep and other resources necessary for good health. Pray for the funds to pay for "extras" like dental and eye care, vitamins and supplements.

DAY 28. FAITH

Trusting in God and His goodness can be the sustaining lifeline for caregivers in times of confusion and crisis. However there are many scenarios that seem utterly hopeless. There are times when it appears God has forgotten or abandoned a family as they try desperately to cope with impossible situations.

Pray families will find themselves refreshed by God's faithfulness. Pray He will show them sparks of redemptive grace along the way that can reassure them of His presence, love and active care. Pray others will come alongside them and remind them of God's mercy and care.

DAY 29. GOOD COUNSEL

Both caregivers and the loved ones they care for need wise input from clergy, friends, family, mental health professionals, legal representatives and medical personnel. However, the counsel they are given can be uninformed or inadequate. Sometimes there are conflicting suggestions or recommendations that are good but just not achievable.

Ask God to help caregivers find knowledgeable advisors. Pray they will be able to sift through the ideas and information from others and recognize what is truly helpful. Pray families will have the energy and insight to follow through on good counsel.

DAY 30. LEGAL ISSUES

Mania, psychosis and other mental health conditions can lead to entanglement with law enforcement and periods of incarceration. In fact, 24% of state prisoners have a recent history of mental illness. Caregivers often find the legal system a maze of confusion and mystery.

Pray God will lead families to compassionate, competent and caring attorneys, judges and law enforcement officers. Pray responses and outcomes will always be what is best for the one struggling with the mental health difficulties. Pray for those who are incarcerated to be protected and to be swiftly released to medical care.

DAY 31. PRAYER

Like Aaron and Hur who helped Moses keep his arms raised during the battle with the Amalekites,* friends of caregivers give tremendous help when they come alongside to share the burden of prayer, especially during times of crisis. Knowing that others are praying for their loved one when they have run out of words or energy is a great comfort to families.

Ask God to raise up intercessors who are dedicated to pray fervently and faithfully for caregivers and their families. Ask Him to show you how to pray for specific situations.

---

*"But Moses' hands grew weary, so they took a stone and put it under him, and he sat on it, while Aaron and Hur held up his hands, one on one side, and the other on the other side. So his hands were steady until the going down of the sun." Exodus 17:12 ESV

ABOUT THE AUTHOR

This prayer guide was written under a pseudonym, Catherine, to help protect the privacy of the family. Identifying details are kept to a minimum for the same reason.

Catherine is also author of the book and blog, *Sparks of Redemptive Grace: Seeking and Seeing God Amid a Loved One's Mental Illness.*

Having served as a missionary for over 25 years, Catherine now works as an independent communications consultant for faith-based nonprofits. She is active in her church as a Bible study leader, intercessor, and mentor to women on issues of faith and faithfulness.

Trained as a teacher for NAMI Family-to-Family classes and facilitator for Grace Alliance support groups, Catherine is an advocate for mental health services and legislation.

**Sparks of
Redemptive Grace:**
*Seeking and Seeing God amid a
Loved One's Mental Illness*

by Catherine P. Downing

Mental illness impacts one out of five families each year, yet few are willing to expose the anguish and tumult they face daily. Informational, devotional, educational, and inspirational, *Sparks of Redemptive Grace* provides an authentic view of one family's transparent hope in God's unfailing love, forged in the fires of fear and faith. Each of the brief 14 chapters overflows with insight, hope, Scriptures and prayers.

For those whose loved one struggles with mental illness, you will find Catherine Downing has told your own story with sincerity and humility. She reminds you of the light of God's goodness that the darkness of mental illness cannot overcome.

For friends watching the chaos surrounding such struggles and wanting to understand, this book will open your eyes not only to the family's needs, but also to the presence of God in their midst. For clergy and counselors looking for resources to support families in crisis, *Sparks of Redemptive Grace* offers comforting truths about God's very real presence in times of trouble.

Sparks of Redemptive Grace is available through your local bookstore and online booksellers.

Subscribe to Catherine's reflective blog:
sparksofredemptivegrace.com/subscribe

For current family resources related to mental health and faith, follow us at:
facebook.com/sparksofredemptivegrace/
twitter.com/sparks_of_grace

www.ingramcontent.com/pod-product-compliance
Lightning Source LLC
Chambersburg PA
CBHW060630030426
42337CB00018B/3283